Business for the Soul

*The Social Entrepreneur's
Step-by-Step Guide to Success*

by
Chris Bouchard

CONTENTS

3

PREFACE

Social entrepreneurs throughout the world are creating a revolution on the approaches they are taking to problem-solving in areas such as the environment, healthcare, education, poverty, and social justice.

They are actively involved in changing the world as they understand that social entrepreneurship is an essential aspect of an organization's business plan. The importance of social entrepreneurship cannot be overstated since it connects the organization to its purpose, keeps it motivated and helps it connect with its consumers.

Social entrepreneurship has become a common pursuit for anyone with a purpose driven venture. People are aware that problems exist in society and want to have a positive impact on the world. A whopping 94% of young people hope to use their skills to contribute to a cause; evidence of an upward trend in social accountability.

As a social entrepreneur myself, I discovered fulfillment lies in extending a helping hand to my fellow human beings and their surroundings. This insight established in me a strong desire to serve, even prompting the operation of a transitional living service before going full-time as a consultant for non-profit organizations and social entrepreneurs; helping with fundraising, program development and planning, evaluation and sustainability, and marketing services.

It is my sincere hope that this book will aid in your approach to social entrepreneurship and in your journey to transform the world.

SECTION 1: SOCIAL ENTREPRENEURSHIP IN THE NON-PROFIT WORLD

Social entrepreneurship has devised effective ways to integrate business strategies into the non-profit sector. This upcoming field is rapidly developing and is also attracting attention from various other sectors. Social entrepreneurship is capable of initiating a social change, and it is that potential remuneration, with its lasting, transformational advantages to the society, that attracts people.

Whether it's a bake shop whose proceeds are used to offset administrative expenses or a well-established micro-lending enterprise, the social entrepreneurial project spectrum is epic. These ventures can be on a small or large scale, unsophisticated or complex.

A ministry that endeavors to train its staff on business practices makes use of social entrepreneurial practices. For example, a finance company that runs various business training programs for its staff, by all means is running a social entrepreneurial program.

Who is the Social Entrepreneur?

A social entrepreneur is someone who has identified a social problem, and then makes use of entrepreneurial principles to establish a venture which best brings about social change. Such a mission could just as well be referred to as a social venture.

Social entrepreneurs have innovative solutions to society's pressing community-based problems. Such individuals are set apart by their aggressive nature and persistence in tackling major issues and brainstorming new ideas.

Since the early 2000s, practitioners have disagreed on the definition of the term, social entrepreneurs. Therefore, we cannot give an affirmative definition because various types of organizations, disciplines, and fields are associated with fulfilling social missions. This includes for-profit organizations, hybrid institutions that combine charitable works with business, non-profit establishments as well as voluntary organizations and NGOs. Environmentalists, social activists, philanthropists, and other socially inclined people are regarded as social entrepreneurs. Different professional backgrounds and types of careers can also be included within the spectrum of the definition of a social entrepreneur.

The modern society has a more altruistic form of social entrepreneurship whose focus is on the benefits reaped by the society. In other words, entrepreneurship translates into a social activity when it's able to transform social capital in such a way that the society is positively impacted. Social entrepreneurship's success is reliant on many factors that are not prioritized by traditional corporate businesses.

Instead of letting the government or corporate segments deal with community needs, these individuals recognize the issues and try to fix them by making changes to the system, ensuring that the solution reaches as many people as possible and persuading society to take new leaps.

Social entrepreneurs have such a high level of determination and commitment to their ideas that it can easily be termed as an obsession. Social entrepreneurs are often so committed to their beliefs that they are ready to change the course of their lives to see their idea implemented. They are often not only visionary but also realistic and concerned with the practical implementation of their vision.

The ideas presented by each social entrepreneur are usually ethical, understandable, user-friendly and have an extensive support base which ensures that people will be more likely to implement it. In simpler terms, any social entrepreneur focuses on the mass recruitment of other change makers who are passionate about the same ideas.

The basic idea of social entrepreneurship is that there is no profit earning and is rather focused on implementing general improvements in the society. But again, any social entrepreneur understands that he/she must be financially and business savvy to find success in this noble cause.

On the other hand, the major motivating factor for most business entrepreneurs is usually the pursuit of profit, which should not be a stumbling block in the social entrepreneur's desire to impact society positively.

Social entrepreneurs have a variety of measuring metrics. Unlike their counterparts, who are gauged mainly on profit or non-profit goals, their aim is to create a positive influence in the society. Typically, it is in the interest of social entrepreneurs to advance cultural, social, and environmental goals that are dominant in the voluntary sector in areas like community development, health care, and poverty alleviation.

Social entreprenuership is a relatively new business model. The term itself gained momentum in 2010, thanks to the internet, specifically social media and social networking. The internet makes it possible for social entrepreneurs to expand their reach to people who are geographically separate but share the same goals. (We will have an in-depth look at this later).

Legal Structures for Social Business

Organizations involved in social entrepreneurship include well-known companies such as pioneer micro-lending institutes with strong roots in the social ladder and corporations that support institutions invested in social and cultural advancement such as hospitals, education facilities, and research projects.

These are the pioneering institutions that are bringing a change to the world of social business. They have managed to alter the institutional structures and create entirely new social industries, showing that it is possible to incorporate social entrepreneurial practices within normal business operations.

Social entrepreneurship is a broad concept. It is a process involving the innovative use and combination of resources to pursue opportunities to catalyze social change and/or address social needs.

For-Profit Company

There are times when the benefits of establishing a profit-making social enterprise become apparent, thus boosting the social goals of an organization. For example, an institution that offers housing and employment to the homeless may establish a restaurant with the intention of both raising money and employing the homeless. Hence, the concept of social enterprise can also apply to for-profit organizations with a strong social bottom line.

One emerging type of association that puts mission first and profits second is the low-profit limited liability company (L3C). Similar to for-profit corporations, the L3C companies pay taxes on profits and can't receive traditional grants or tax-deductible charitable contributions. Private foundations will be permitted to make program-related investments (PRIs) to these companies once it is reviewed and approved by IRS. The L3C is a new legal structure that has already been approved in some states however legislation is still pending in many states.

What exactly is a for-profit company within the context of social entrepreneurship?

A for-profit company can be defined as an institution that earns profit through its operations for its own advancement as opposed to a public corporation. This is an organization operating in the private sector.

The public can purchase shares of ownership in the company, and the owners of these shares are what we call the shareholders. They give a certain amount of money for a particular portion of ownership in the company. What's more, they are not aided by the government and work towards financial gains. Profit-making is their number one goal.

The system has been structured in such a way that the for-profit corporations must register with the state and pay applicable taxes. Any donations are also taxable depending on the country's fiscal policies. Considering that these companies usually have a separate identity from their owners, the proprietors are not legally bound to pay any debt the company may owe.

From a traditional point of view, the for-profit company is solely focused on ensuring that its investors get maximum returns. On the other hand, the non-profit company is only meant to serve the public's interest.

But modern for-profit corporations have learned that the best way to have a good public image is to share some of the enormous profits they make with society. That is why large profit-oriented corporations turn to social entrepreneurship as a way of projecting a positive image. Social entrepreneurship is something that is yet to be fully embraced by the organizations. The fact that different investors are brought on board can make it more challenging. Making too much mission talk with professional investors may be challenging for someone who wants you to focus just on the business. Many corporates tend to flee from the perceived 'do-gooders' who are likely to be less focused on bringing a return on the invested money.

Some for-profit companies make their money from service to the public. One such example is an online grocer that takes produce directly from the farmer and delivers it to your doorstep. The service allows people to gain access to locally produced fresh foods, and with proper food, the company can make the world a better place.

Non-profit

A non-profit organization (NPO) is one whose intentions are not solely focused on making profits. Rather, the emphasis is on a social cause or a particular point of view. Economically speaking, a non-profit would use its surplus revenues to continue with its mission, which is not distributed amongst the organization's equivalent of shareholders as dividends or profits. In other words, there is the non-distribution constraint.

Nonprofit organizations enjoy certain privileges that are granted as a boon to them, in exchange for abiding by laws that limit the use of the association's assets and require governance by a board. Nonprofit establishments may have different agendas, but they all share the same general purpose. Unlike for-profit businesses, nonprofits are designed to benefit society tangibly. From a layman's perception, the terms non-profit and not-for-profit can be similar in meaning. However, there is a difference in some jurisdictions, as there may be legal and accounting differences. People start nonprofit organizations to tackle social problems. While professionals, such as doctors or lawyers, set up nonprofits to promote their profession, institute standards and provide opportunities for professional development.

An organization may decide to operate as a non-profit and obtain tax exemption or charitable status. However, the IRS requires that any organization applying for tax exemption (under section 501c3) must be organized for one or more charitable purposes, including educational, religious, public safety testing, scientific, promotion of literacy, amateur sports, or the prevention of child or animal abuse.

The evolution of social entrepreneurship has made it difficult to draw the line between NPOs and charitable organizations because they have been used interchangeably for quite some time. However, charities are set apart by the fact that they tend to consume a bigger chunk of the private non-profit sector.

The non-profits are usually classified into either community-serving or member-serving organizations. The former is focused on offering services to the community either locally or globally. These organizations provide development programs, human service programs, and health, educational and medical research services. The member-serving NPOs, on the other hand, include trade unions, respective societies, cooperatives, sports clubs, retired servicemen's clubs, industry associations, credit unions and peak bodies. These are the kind of organizations that concentrate on meeting the needs of a given group of people, which is, the organization's members.

Non-profit organizations often face the challenge of hiring and retaining skilled staff, due to a limitation of funds to offer competitive salaries. They often employ young, ambitious college graduates who serve for a short time to gain experience, before they accept higher paying positions elsewhere.

Public Benefits Corporation or B Corporation

The Benefit Corporation is a unique type of for-profit entity that positively impacts society, the environment, workers, and the community, while pursuing profit as a legally defined goal. They are mainly created with the purpose of providing a general public benefit, striving to achieve maximum positive and minimum negative impact.

Just like a traditional corporation, the Benefit Corporation's directors hold the same authority but are legally bound to make decisions that will not only benefit their shareholders but the environment as well. A B Corporation is differentiated from a Certified Corporation in its transparency, accountability, and purpose. The two identities have similar taxation obligations.

Social entrepreneurs often opt to join a B Corporation to mirror their environmental goals and fiduciary responsibility. The creation of a B Corporation is a public commitment to the creation of a positive impact on the society and the environment while the laws governing the business world still hold. A hired independent entity develops the third-party standards. This entity must not have a financial relationship with the B Corporation and must have the expertise to assess the company's performance through the multi-stakeholder approach.

People tend to associate corporations with business, but historically speaking, they were introduced to serve a given public purpose. Their history is deeply rooted in subdivisions within the government as well as religion. The institution is independent of the mortality of its members. For instance, if a member dies, the corporation does not die with him/her.

The significant difference between a non-profit organization and a benefit corporation—is the ownership aspect. There are no shareholders in a not-for-profit company while a B Corporation does have stakeholders who own the company.

A nonprofit company usually aims to serve a public benefit without making a profit, as defined by the IRS and if the organization decides to stop doing business and close, it must distribute its assets to other non-profits. Such organizations aren't owned by anyone because there aren't any shareholders. However, a benefit corporation is owned by shareholders who expect the company to make a profit and return some of that money to them as dividends.

The Certificate of Incorporation of a Benefit Corporation requires that the organization spend some of its profits or resources (or both) in support of a specific public benefit. If a C corporation decides to end its business and shut down, the shareholders receive the proceeds of the sales of assets, after liabilities are paid. The shareholders of a benefit corporation actually own the company as well as its assets.

An annual report is a required filing for B Corporations to indicate how their performance had social and environmental benefits. As much as some may view this to be a hassle, the B Corporation has a marketing advantage as opposed to the

C Corporation as through their social responsibility; they can market their services in a more appealing manner, meaning that they are more likely to attract more consumers. Further on, customers demonstrate their prioritization of ethics every time they make a purchase.

However, the fact that Benefit Corporations file an annual report places them in a position where they may encounter more transaction costs than their peers. The requirement to maintain a given level of transparency on its ability to meet its social responsibility does not lower the costs.

Benefit Corporations give social entrepreneurs and directors an opportunity to run a company on behalf of the shareholders and the community. This is a golden opportunity in today's era where consumers seem to prefer businesses that embrace social responsibility increasingly.

It is common to have a situation where individuals are unable to draw the parallels between Benefit Corporations and Certified Corporations. These two are complimentary and have lots of similarities. They also have important differences which will be discussed below.

The Benefit Corporations are available in only 30 states within the U.S., whereas the C Corporations are available to every business regardless of their state, country, or business structure. The performance of the B Corporation is self-reported while that of the C Corporation must meet the least verified score. Also, recertification every two years is necessary. Similarly, the cost of establishing a B Corporation is more compared to their counterparts.

Philanthropy-based organizations

A philanthropy-based organization is a type of non-profit organization. It's differentiated from the other types of NPOs in the sense that it is centered on charitable goals in addition to championing for social well-being.

Different countries have varying legal definitions of a philanthropic organization, and in some cases, the definition may differ depending on the group's location. There is also a variation in the regulation, tax treatment, and charity laws.

The sustainability of a charitable organization is measured in terms of its financial figures by the charity evaluators. The information obtained has an impact on the charitable establishment's donors and thus the organization's financial goals.

A section of the charitable organization's finances usually comes from for-profit organization's donations, which is a part of a bigger part of corporate philanthropy.

The philanthropy-based organization usually gives out receipts to donors, which can be used to reduce income tax. They have a structure that differs from that of the for-profit organizations as they include unpaid positions held by volunteers. Because they have a variety of income sources, there must be a mechanism for managing this revenue and ensuring that it's used for the intended purpose.

The Board of Directors manage the philanthropic organization and the current law demands at least three directors, to incorporate most of its jurisdictions. The directors are the founders; they adopt the organization's bylaws and use a majority vote to decide on policies and the mode of operation.

The laws explicitly state how a person can join the Board of Directors, the manner in which meetings are called, what makes up a quorum and the election of the organization's officers. These directors are volunteers and do not partake of any surplus.

The Staff

The workload in many organizations may be too much for the managers alone to handle, that's why they need volunteers to help them out. The organization may employ a manager who has a budget to hire staff. The team must be organized in such a way that it creates room for volunteers to conduct their duties unhampered. The structure emphasizes the importance of volunteers, just as it values the paid staff members.

Mode of operation

Many philanthropic organizations are engaged in various activities such as offering goods and services, to generate extra income. Although these establishments are not profit-oriented, the structure in many cases resembles for-profit organizations. The manager oversees the operations, while the staff handles the sales and deliveries and reports to the manager, who in turn presents his information to the Board of Directors.

SECTION 2: FUNDING YOUR SOCIAL ENTERPRISE

Financial reserves and the proper investment of said finances are increasingly becoming an important matter for social entrepreneurs. Investing can be a challenging decision, and in particular for the social entrepreneur running a non-profit organization. The fact that they strive to tackle societal issues does not necessarily mean that they have excellent investment strategies. The for-profit social entrepreneur, on the other hand, knows how to disburse their funds accurately. Thus, their success is reliant on how innovative they are when it comes to investment and the acquirement of potential sources of funds.

A mission-driven social entrepreneurship venture is bound to grow– which in essence can be a blessing and a curse at the same time. It is a curse as growth leads to a demand for more capital, which, if mishandled, can jeopardize the entire mission.

Investors and Capital

Many social entrepreneurs are faced with the challenge of scouring the market for the capital needed to start and expand their social enterprise or proceed with their projects. There are different types of social companies and investors. Mutual understanding helps to find the right match.

According to research on pwc.com – a trusted research and insights site, investors admit that social impact and profit are mutually beneficial. They would prefer giving their money to a social enterprise that states its vision for the society as well as the financial gains. Drifting from the mission potentially risks crippling the social enterprise.

'Regular' businesses also have their struggles accessing capital, but this can be more challenging for social entrepreneurs because they have to align their financial needs with their social responsibilities.

It is essential to find a good match between a social enterprise and its potential investor. Some stakeholders have their own unique way in which they approach risk, financial and social return. Similarly, social entrepreneurs' definition of financial and social factors may be different from the norm. It may seem obvious to define what the organization offers, but it's crucial to have a deeper understanding of this before approaching a list of potential investors.

Most pioneers are passionate. Having an idea – a big one, in fact – is just a drop in the ocean. The primary task is securing funding because, without it, the whole idea may crumble. The initial backing, in many cases, can be easy to source by the assistance of family and friends.

But what follows after this?

Over 90 percent of social enterprises studied by Intellecap confirmed that they relied on funding for their missions. The sources of funding can vary depending on the idea's maturity, the type of legal structure and the startup's stage.

Some of the ways you can pursue funding and grow your social business include:

- Public Funding

- Grant writing

- Fee for service

- Fundraising

Each of these sources has particular governance issues.

Public Funding

From an economic point of view, public funds refer to money that the government generates so that it can provide goods and services. Public funding is applicable both in the business sector and in politics. For instance, a qualified presidential candidate receives federal government funds for campaign expenses.

There are many public funding options that a social entrepreneur can access. Earmarked funds and public charities exist for the sole purpose of advancing the best interest of society and allocation of that money is not always limited to other municipalities, state, or federal agencies. At no time should anyone get the impression that there is no money as money is always available.

Grant Writing

Grant writing involves gathering documentation and fulfilling requirements of various funding bodies to pursue funding on behalf of the client/agency formally. Writing a proposal and submitting that proposal to apply for a grant opportunity is often referred to as grant writing.

While working on a grant, it is important to tune the language so as to align it with the given context and to keep in mind the quality of language, tone, and details expected by the institution offering the grant. A bigger part of successful grant writing is reliant on a deeper understanding of the process of creating a grant proposal. The components of a grant proposal are as follows:

- Analyze the target audience to whom the proposal will be presented;

- Analyze the project's purpose;

- Collect sufficient information regarding the proposal's subject;

- Select the relevant type of proposal – in our case; it is a grant proposal;

- Write down the proposal;

- Format it officially;

- Revise, edit and proofread your writings; and

- Submit the grant application.

Once the writer, the executive board and the team assembled for the project have crafted the proposal and established all its details, the proceeding steps involve listing the specific outcomes anticipated. This list lets the writer highlight the order in which the outcomes are to be realized and the details in each section. While listing the expected results, it is important to clearly outline the manner in which the donor is likely to be impacted.

The proposal writing process should be accompanied by a hand-in-hand drafting and formatting of the steps involved. The grant writer should always prepare the submission following the proposal requirements.

The proposal's structure is determined by the type of project, the organization as well as the type of proposal.

The overall structure will include the following sections:

- Summary

- Introduction

- Plan of work

- Budget

- Experience

- Appendixes

The summary will contain the main components of your proposal. This section needs to be short but explicit in the sense that it describes the problem/opportunity, solution, timeline, outcomes, costs, and qualifications.

The introduction outlines the proposal as well as its scope and gives information about the organization. Typically, it should have a brief description of the problem which is also referred to as the "statement of need." The introduction also needs to describe the purpose, source of information, organization of the proposal, and the key terms used. It is important to have the key terms in the introduction so the grant committee will not get confused when reading the proposal.

The plan of work presents the solution to the identified problem. If the project needs some research, this section can be used to outline the research requirements in the proposal. This segment also needs to highlight the expected outcomes. A successful plan is one that has measurable results.

The budget section outlines the proposal's expenses. This section needs to ensure costs highlighted are reasonable and go hand-in-hand with the expected outcomes. You may find it helpful to make a separation between direct costs spent on travel, salaries, supplies, and the necessary materials and indirect costs – intangible costs.

The qualifications and experience section identifies clearly the suitability of the people engaged in planning the work. The details required to be included in this section are dependent on the complexity of the project.

The appendixes present the proposal in terms of charts and graphics. Some other documents that can be included in this section are support letters and testimonials. It is an added advantage if the letters of support come from well-known and respected people and organizations.

After submitting the grant application, additional steps may be required, such as the applicant organization making a follow-up contact. Some institutions and government departments may undertake a site visit before making a decision regarding the proposal. This makes it essential to ensure a high level of professionalism at all times.

Fee for Service

This model of a social enterprise promotes its social services and then sells them to the target audience, which includes individuals, firms, communities, or third parties.

This classic technique is fixed: the social program itself is the business. The social mission goals are fulfilled by the organization by providing social services in the sector it works in, for example, the healthcare sector, the education sector, etc. The social enterprise earns revenue through fees charged for services, which is then used to recover the expenditures that were used to deliver the service, daily expenses, marketing outlays and much more. Surpluses may be used to support social enterprises that do not have a cost-recovery mechanism in place.

The fee-for-service is frequently used by non-profits to support their social programs. Membership organizations, museums, universities, and hospitals are typical examples of fee-for-service social enterprises.

For example, the fee charged by schools for its educational services is used by the institution to reimburse costs such as teachers' salaries and maintenance. Therefore, there are never enough funds available for the establishment of new facilities or academic research centers. In such situations, institutions tend to supplement the tuition income with an additional fee-for-service enterprise.

This type of a social enterprise may also be termed as an earned income venture. By selling goods or services, a nonprofit organization can expand its funding base while creating a positive impact in the community. Therefore, most non-profit organizations earn income by selling products and providing services to the public, various agencies, and service users. For some organizations, their entire revenue is made exclusively through the selling of goods and services.

Not all non-profits depend on donors for their revenue. Instead, they sell services or products to support their mission. In the case of a large institution such as a hospital or a university, there are a lot of opportunities to earn revenue through health care service charges and tuition fees.

Philanthropic organizations often set up a distinct trading arm so that the team can continue to focus on its primary aim.

Any non-profit offering services for a fee needs to be aware of a few important factors such as the Unrelated Business Income Tax (UBIT). Any service you offer has to be in line with the mission defined in the organization's official document. If it isn't, then the revenue earned can be subjected to the UBIT. For those works that may include the training given to the disadvantaged among the people you serve, such revenue collected will not come under UBIT laws.

Charging a fee for a service can be administered in a variety of ways. For example, if you help the unemployed secure a job, you can charge a service fee. Similarly, a non-profit music academy or preschool may charge a fee for teaching interested persons.

But service fee charged on a large scale may turn out to be a nightmare for you. Therefore, it is important that you consider these questions before you take a significant step that might harm your mission.

- What does the governing document permit regarding trading activities?

- Will the trade pose a large risk to the organization?

- Does the investment opportunity synchronize with the organization's investment policies?

Besides charging a fee for services provided, some non-profits may appeal for 'voluntary' donations. In such a case, a user is offered a service and then asked to give a gift rather than be charged a fee. You will commonly notice a donation box in such organizations, often at the entrance.

This is a good way to raise funds, but the organization should not coerce anyone into giving a contribution. A donation, according to its definition, must be made voluntarily.

Fundraising

The saying – "money is king," holds true for any business including non-profits. Nonprofit organizations survive on funds without which it's difficult to run all the programs that the company intends to engage in. Unlike the for-profit business, non-profits are not obliged to promise investors or their equivalent a return on their money, and neither can the organization expect to make a profit from sales.

One option that you can easily turn to for revenue raising is donations. The social entrepreneur can approach foundations and government subsections as well as corporations for grants. If the entrepreneur is capable of creating a name for themself or the organization among influential people, that will surely help in gaining enormous donations.

Seeking donations is known as fundraising. Two basic commandments govern fundraising: be simple and be focused. Many non-profits find it difficult to raise money because they tend to chase every conceivable opportunity and in the process, they dilute their effort and lose sight of the primary goal.

Fundraising entails any act aimed at attracting donations into the non-profit. These actions include efforts to get cash or in-kind donations from individuals, philanthropists, and grant-making agencies.

Most startup social entrepreneurs lack a wider source of donations, the core ones being special events and individuals. In some rare cases, they may manage to attract government funding for a particular program.

Once an organization is established and more well-known, they can apply for philanthropic donations. Individuals in charge of donations from these groups consider an excellent record of accomplishment, as well as good management, to be sure that their donations will be put to productive use and aid in meeting their philanthropic goals. Typically, startups do not have a track record of proven success, which is often a barrier to their initiatives to attract charitable donations.

Beginning a fundraising campaign can be as simple as developing a case statement. All that is needed is a one or two-page case statement explaining to the prospective donors how you intend to use their money to make an impact on the target community. It is vital to have the case statement because it forms the basis of the donation, offers collateral material, and ensures the non-profit's message is presented consistently. Having an unclear case statement may result in a muddled message.

Questions addressed in a case statement

- What is the major issue that needs to be resolved? (This is an expansion of the mission statement).

- What are the intended outcomes? (Outcomes need to be measurable).

- What sets your organization apart?

- What steps will you follow to achieve the program and service goals?

- What accomplishments has the organization made to date? (People generally prefer to take part in fundraisers organized by successful organizations).

Leveraging Resources

An unstable economy always challenges the survival of a non-profit organization. During times of countrywide financial crisis, nonprofit organizations witness a decrease in donations and usually have a lack of capital to support their programs. Often these economic setbacks lead to greater competition in the non-profit sector, with many organizations contending for the same sources that can provide funding. Owing to this type of economic environment, shortage of cash is one problem that many social entrepreneurs compete with. By taking a creative approach of using existing resources, the organization may be surprised at how much it can achieve.

The following are four effective ways to leverage resources:

Creative Marketing: Marketing is the most basic tool that can be used to earn revenue at a time of need. Social media is a phenomenal place to run a marketing campaign, understand the needs of your customers and prospect, and then concentrate the promotion of your organization/product/service toward that end. By determining the interests of your clients, you can set yourself apart as an expert in the given field.

Crowdfunding: Crowdfunding can be a way of raising money without the involvement of lawyers, regulatory agencies, and bankers. Crowdfunding is not a new technique but one that has gained the attention of entrepreneurs and investors alike through highly publicized platforms on the internet. You can reach the public online through various sites such as Indiegogo, GoFundMe, and Kickstarter.

In-Kind Donations: Many times, corporations would rather provide cashless payments. Such noncash contributions may include product donations, event tickets or even free airtime.

Before declining, consider the probability of their goods being more valuable than if they paid cash. If you cannot use the given item/return service/favor, you may be able to leverage it to your advantage. In this case, you may get yourself a loyal and happy customer as well as an item that may prove useful to your mission.

Measuring Social Media: Always monitor your social media to determine how your subscribers react to your activities. Whether Facebook, Twitter, Instagram, LinkedIn or other similar pages, make sure that you have a team working to improve your posts and your public image, around the clock. In this 21st century, your image on social media can either rocket your business to the sky or burn it down completely. It is also important to go through each comment and the analyze social media feedback to understand how you can be more efficient in promoting your business.

Marketing

One of the best ways to grow your support base is through marketing.

The following are some key marketing tips:

- Speak to at least three people daily about the organization's mission and goals. Do not follow the HAP method (Hope and Pray) wherein entrepreneurs sit at their offices, behind their computers and expect someone to appear and invest in their programs magically.

- Perform research on prime locations where your target audience spends most of their time. Get out and meet them. Tell them about your organization, what it does and explain to them your goals and objectives.

- Be an active social network person. Start conversations, join in discussions with others, offer help and share ideas.

- Always follow up on anything that you have begun. This is what, over time, turns a connection into a client who later may bring funds or other benefits to your organization.

- Communicate the key aspects of your enterprise precisely and be confident in your communication.

The sine qua non of social entrepreneurship lies in the capability to balance between social impact and financial viability. One can easily regard social entrepreneurs as tightrope walkers. These are individuals juggling between their social responsibility and the realities of the marketplace.

Different organizations have a different definition of the term 'appropriate,' and many social entrepreneurs are often challenged when they have to choose among the kinds of products and services to offer and the market segments to focus on, while also ensuring that they comply with the organization's values.

Rather than exerting your efforts to be a Jack of all Trades, it is best to focus on a carefully chosen area where you have a high chance of excelling. Failure to do so will undoubtedly lead to a situation where the organization is unable to pay vital attention to customer needs.

This advice is in sharp contrast to how a lot of traditional non-profits operate. Many non-profit managers are guilty of having tried to sell various products and offer services at the same time. Their morph into social entrepreneurship often hits them with the hard reality that contraction is the key to success.

Social entrepreneurs can serve more people better than ever before, simply by cutting down on the number of products and the target market. They allow themselves the resources and the time to maximize on the areas in which they excel.

Comparative View on Traditional and Modern Marketing

Marketing entails communicating to your potential buyers the value of a given good or service with the objective of selling it to them.

With new marketing opportunities now available via the internet and social media, it is interesting to note what has changed over the years.

Traditional marketing involved the advertisement of the brand or organization in magazines and newspapers, television and radios, catalogs, brochures, newsletters, billboards, telemarketing, and direct mail.

The traditional method was useful in its time as it was literally the only way customers could be contacted. But then came the internet with access to a worldwide audience. What's more, data mining meant we could customize the products that different people saw online!

The very first difference between the two techniques is that with traditional marketing, priority is given to selling the product. Marketing and product selling is almost inseparable as in both the cases; the primary focus is to gain a profit.

Modern marketing, on the other hand, aims at customer satisfaction and building a relationship with the same set of activities used to depict a deeper understanding of the client's wants and desires regarding the product and organization.

Traditional marketing

- The company is individually involved in organizing the product and promoting it using conventional methods, such as radio and TV, newspaper and magazines, other printed materials, and telemarketing.

- The focus is on generating more sales for a higher profit.

Modern Marketing

- Modern Marketing tends to be more internet-based and seeks to build a relationship with the customers.

- Buyers can easily compare product prices on different websites.

- Some of the online mediums for advertising include Facebook, Pinterest, Pay Per Click, Content Marketing, and Banner Advertisements on websites.

The fact that Modern Marketing has taken the advertising sphere by storm does not mean that traditional methods of marketing are obsolete. Traditional marketing still works but it's more effective when combined with internet-based marketing.

SECTION 3: DIGITAL MARKETING FOR THE SOCIAL ENTREPRENEUR

Social entrepreneurs who set out to combat some of the most challenging situations in society can make use of digital marketing to spread their word across their target market segment. Social media platforms such as LinkedIn, Twitter, Facebook, Pinterest, Instagram and Google Plus offer an opportunity for real-time interaction between the organization and their customers.

The following are some of the ways social entrepreneurs can utilize internet marketing to promote their social enterprise:

Have your goals set: The very first strategy in developing any form of advertisement is identifying your outcome for the campaign. This is what helps you formulate strategy and make decisions. Do you want to create awareness, improve your credibility or attract a broader customer base?

Select your preferred channels: Digital marketing offers several channels that the social entrepreneur can use to achieve the identified goals. Twitter is News inclined; Facebook connects people with their interests while Google Plus advocates for collaboration. A blog uses content to market your organization while Facebook Advertisements can be targeted to specific people with specific interests in specific geographical areas. Select a method that best suits your organizational needs and goals.

Have appropriate content: Create engaging and relevant content for your audience. Include keywords that can be easily picked up by search engines.

Social Media

Social media is a magic wand for any entrepreneur that does away with traditional marketing altogether. It is not only a tool used to gain exposure but is an investment that can yield bucket loads of revenue for your organization. The term social media refers to all sites that offer social actions – which vary from one social media site to another. Twitter, for instance, focuses on short messages and news updates while Facebook allows unlimited content length in addition to photo and video sharing. Instagram, on the other hand, is about sharing visual and audio content – photos and videos.

You can tie in advertisements and promote your organization and its services on your Facebook page and Twitter. With so many people now using these platforms, social media has become the go-to choice for marketers. An organization is now able to share its message with its targeted audience with ease and at a lower cost than ever before.

Tips for effective social media marketing:

- Attract an audience. Develop compelling and relevant content, join in conversations, and contribute on useful topics, to increase your reputation on social media.

- Analyze how past posts have performed. Many different tools can be used to analyze social media to give an insight into what posts were popular among customers.

- Integrate links into the visual content.

The success of marketing via social media depends on the quality of posts. Be patient. Success will not happen overnight. It can take weeks and months of planning to achieve the desired results. And once the results are achieved, maintaining the highest standard is important.

Online Events

Event marketing involves developing a themed exhibit or presentation with the intention of driving attention towards an organization, a cause, product, or service. The event can be online or offline, sponsored or self-hosted. A successful online event is one that manages to get people to participate and take the action you have identified.

You can market your organization, product, services as well as your mission by hosting webinars, language classes and group discussions online. Initially, start with a few free classes moving on to a payment fee. Various organizations hold online gaming challenges, quizzes, and even workshops. Make sure that your online events are exciting and invigorating so as to attract more people to join your events. With this approach, not only can you promote your mission but you will be able to earn revenue from your marketing.

How do you motivate your followers to market the online event on your behalf and reach a wider audience?

Contests can create a buzz. As an example, you can encourage people to share a given photo and hashtag it. In exchange, they stand to win a given reward depending on how many likes their picture gets. You can offer VIP experiences or free tickets. Social media can always do the trick. So, post about your online event on all social media sites to start raising awareness at least a month before the scheduled date.

Make use of influencer marketing to get publicity. Make a different request to the influencers in your field because chances are you are not the only one seeking their attention. Draft a personalized request to at least 20 influencers that operate within your area of interest. Motivate the influencers by giving them a reason to care. You can pay affiliates to do the marketing for you.

If your online event spans out for a couple of days, then make sure that you end each day's event with a promise of a surprise for the next day so that your participants do not drop out from the event after a day. An online event needs to be memorable. Its format will be determined by your goals and should provide useful information. It should not just be an advertisement for your organization. Host engaging events which will allow people to interact with the members of your organization.

Email Marketing

Email marketing involves sending commercial messages via email. This marketing technique has been used since the dawn of the email.

Email marketing can be used in many ways, including the following:

Newsletters: This is one of the best ways to maintain a lasting relationship with your customers and attract prospects. Email newsletters are possibly one of the best ways to stay in contact with your clients on a daily, weekly, or monthly basis. Customers do not like junk so do not fill their inbox folder with daily emails, because this will lead to them unsubscribing from your newsletters. Therefore, most organizations choose to send emails weekly or monthly. However, with high-quality content, daily newsletters also can yield better results.

Event invitations: You can use email marketing to invite people to join your event. Tools for email marketing are highly sophisticated and make it possible to personalize emails. For instance, you can send an email to multiple people, but each person receives an email that begins with their name. It is a way of reducing the costs of printing and posting invitations.

Business updates: Inform your customers about new products and services and offer a free a trial. Send updates about new features and how they are likely to benefit from them.

Blog posts: If your business has a blog, when you add a new post promote it to your customers and prospects. A blog not only helps to create a buzz through followers but can act as a medium that will help you connect with your clients directly. Some people would prefer accessing your blog post via email rather than visiting a website. Send a weekly or monthly summary of all blog posts.

Email marketing is a powerful tool due to its low cost, flexibility, and speed.

Search Engine Optimization and Management

Online users utilize search engines such as Google, Bing, and Yahoo to find information on any given subject. They type in the Search Bar words/terms that are then processed, and the results are presented by the search engine. The words typed in the search bar are called keywords, and the search engine works by comparing what you have typed with millions of websites present on the internet and displays the most relevant sites for that keyword.

The content and videos are usually ranked on their relevance as decided by the search engine. Research shows that results displayed on the first page of the search engine stand a higher chance of being clicked as opposed to websites on other pages. That is why websites are always struggling to emerge on top – either through search engine optimization (SEO), free organic traffic, or search engine marketing (SEM).

When writing an SEO-based post, ensure that keywords are not overused. How do you feel reading a blog post full of repetitive words? Let me guess, you get bored if not angered and eventually decide to leave the site. Your content should be natural. The keywords should be inserted only where appropriate, rather than appear as if they were forced to fit.

You can also register your organization with Google Places, which allows your business to be found more easily on Google searches and will pinpoint the location of your organization on the Google Map. Customers usually like to authenticate the existence of any business via Google Map, and if you are on it, then you pass their first test of verification. For this, you will have to fill out a form and register. Once your organization is verified by the confirmation process (via mail or a phone call), your organization is on the map. There are similar options available with Yahoo! known as Yahoo! Local and Microsoft's Bing.

Pay-Per-Click/Cost-Per-Click Marketing

Pay-Per-Click (PPC) is also referred to as Cost-Per-Click (CPC). It is a method of internet advertising in which the advertiser places an ad on websites and then pays the website owner only when the ad is clicked. Due to its dominance in the internet sphere, PPC/CPC is commonly associated with top search engines like Google and Bing. Social media platforms such as Twitter and Facebook also use the PPC model.

A website that makes use of PPC ads will feature a given advertisement if the keyword is in line with the advertiser's keywords query or if the content site has relevant content. These ads are usually labeled 'sponsored ads' and will appear either above, beneath or adjacent to the organic results as decided by the web developer.

The advertiser determines the monthly budget and the maximum CPC for each keyword. Budgets range from $50 to over $500,000 per month.

CPC begins with setting a daily budget. After reaching the advertiser's daily budget, the ad is hidden for that day.

There are two ways an advertiser can set the amount to pay for each click. The first method is a formula, and the other is via the bidding process. The method used is - the cost per impression (CPI) divided by percent click-through ratio (%CTR).

When the paid advertisement is clicked, the website publisher is usually paid the CPC. With an ever-rising number of online businesses, CPC advertising is becoming a norm. This form of digital marketing can be utilized by the social entrepreneur to achieve their goals and objectives.

Merits of Digital Marketing

The 21st century is the internet era, and anyone not taking advantage of modern marketing opportunities needs to start doing so! The benefits of digital marketing are:

Wider Audience Reach

Internet marketing overcomes geographical barriers, making it possible to sell almost any product in any part of the world without the need to establish local physical outlets. It's even feasible to create an export business without having to open a distribution network in the target country.

24/7 Operation

Digital marketing makes it possible for a company to operate around the clock without worrying about closing hours or overtime. Online selling is convenient for customers. They can browse through the available goods and place an order when it is convenient for them.

Personalization

It is easy to customize the offers made to people by having a well-built customer profile, based on their purchasing history. Technological advancement has made it possible to keep track of customer web visits and activity and then make an offer that reflects their interests. Data obtained from customer web activity is useful in organizing cross-selling campaigns.

Credibility

Having a digital profile is now an essential expectation of businesses. It is a way of building relationships with customers and increases the likelihood of retaining customers. For example, following an online purchase, the customer would receive a 'thank you' email, thus extending the seller-customer link much further than a single purchase. The email may also suggest other products that may be of interest and give information on current offers. This way the customer's interest is piqued and they go on to buy other products from the store.

Cheap Marketing

Digital marketing has reduced the costs of advertising compared to marketing products or services the traditional way.

Return on Investment

Digital marketing gives a measurable return on investment. It is possible to track the profits or actions as a result of marketing and clearly see which techniques produced the best results.

Video marketing, Skype, Webinars, Social Media, and many other methods have provided an opportunity to connect with the world via the internet. This innovative way of reaching your target audience can be efficiently utilized for both, the benefit of the organization and the customer.

SECTION 4: PROJECT MANAGEMENT FOR THE SOCIAL ENTERPRISE

Social entrepreneurship is a rapidly evolving area that continuously transforms the lives of all the stakeholders. The primary intention of social entrepreneurship is to tackle social difficulties via financially-stable business models. This success would be close to impossible without proper management of project initiatives by social enterprises.

A project is a temporary endeavor that has a defined beginning and end, focusing on achieving results. It is constrained by deadlines and the need for funding. Being a temporary initiative, projects are in contrast to the usual business operations which tend to be permanent or semi-permanent and repetitive. These are managed in quite a different way, and most cases require specific technical skills and management strategies.

The biggest challenge any given project faces is the achievement of the overall goal, without which the project can result in a complete failure. The goal should be conveniently achieved notwithstanding the constraints which include time, scope, budget, and quality. In addition to these limitations, additional restrictions are put in place regarding the necessary inputs and achievement of predefined objectives.

The social enterprise may find it a necessity to hire a project manager to take charge. They are usually responsible for planning, execution, controlling and closing the project once its goals have been accomplished.

Vital project management roles may include defining the project objectives, requirements and managing all project constraints. The project manager primarily represents the client – the social enterprise – and must ensure that their needs have been met. The organization may get a qualified individual from within the company to take up the project manager role or may employ a third party to handle the tasks. If an outside person is recruited, his/her ability to quickly adapt to the internal operational structure and closely work with nominated representatives will greatly aid in the success of the project.

It becomes unrealistic if one talks of project management without mentioning project risk management, because a risk management process is absolutely necessary to ensure that your social mission is in not in jeopardy. According to the United States Department of Defense, the four elements used to track program status are schedule, cost, performance, and risk. Some international standards such as ISO 21500: 2012 – Guidance on project management and ISO 31000: 2009 – Risk management, also apply.

Risk management entails proactively identifying the project aspects, the problem(s) it intends to handle and the consequences of given decisions.

Social and regular enterprises are increasingly making use of project portfolio management (PPM) to select the appropriate project and then integrate the project management techniques. The primary objective is to ensure that the intended outcomes are delivered as stated in the project manual. Besides the PPM, project management software is equally and actively used to plan, organize and distribute resources proportionately. The functionality of any given software relies on the level of software sophistication, including general functions such as resource allocation, cost control, scheduling, communication, workflow, risk management, decision making, budget, administration, and documentation. Still within project management is the concept of virtual project management (VVM) in which a virtual team manages the project. Whereas the term may refer to a virtual environment being used to implement a project, the technicalities involved are fundamentally different from those of a traditional project.

Project Life Cycle

Traditionally, a project undergoes five stages during its time, depending on the project management methodology used and they are as follows:

- Initiation

- Planning

- Delivery

- Evaluation

- Closing.

Each of these phases may be supplemented with decision points at which the continuation of a project can be debated.

Initiation: The origin of any given idea lies in a vision. Just the same way a journey of a thousand miles begins with a single a step, a clear vision is the stepping stone for any social enterprise. Where do you see yourself, a few years, if not months down the line? What is the final destination from which you can set new goals? This is the stage at which the relevant team, brainstorms ideas, thinking out of the box until a common ground is reached.

If the initiation stage is not performed correctly, it is highly unlikely that the project will be successful. The major factors to consider at this stage are whether the business environment is well understood and if all the controls have been incorporated in the project. Any deficiencies have to be highlighted and appropriate measures should be taken.

This stage should ensure that the following have been captured:

- Business requirements in measurable goals

- Current operations have been well reviewed

- Financial analysis

- Project stakeholders' analysis

- Project schedules, deliverables, and costs

- SWOT analysis (which determines business strengths, weaknesses, opportunities, and threats)

The organization's blue-sky thinkers lie within the team of initiators (Blue sky thinkers are the people who are never comfortable when restricted). They are idea generators –

often coming up with concepts that others would not have imagined. But the initiator isn't a planner; he/she typically chunks out an idea and needs a planner to take charge of the rest.

Planning: Once you have conceptualized a destination in your mind, a guiding map is a key element to getting there. The planning stage entails seeking detailed answers to tough questions such as the method of attracting funds, roles of the key players, the timescales and defining the responsibilities different teams have.

The planner is a person who pays close attention to details. They are the type of people who ensure that the project is deeply thought out to ensure success. There is no doubt that social enterprises often have a more complex planning structure compared to the regular business. The planning is not just focused on making profit or generating income but also to ensure that the social obligations are fully met. The main goal of this stage is to develop a schedule with regard to time, resources and cost and then to ensure that they are adequately distributed among the different teams that will work on the project. Just like the initiation stage, a hasty and unsure plan is highly likely to lead a project to its downfall. Just as the saying goes, failing to plan is planning to fail!

In general, project planning covers the following:

- Deciding on the planning technique – Rolling Wave planning (the project is planned in 'waves' and becomes clearer as it proceeds) or planning by level of detail.

- Creating the scope/vision statement

- Putting together the planning team

- Estimating the cost and time

- Risk planning

- Drafting the budget

- Developing measures for quality assurance

- Determining the required resources

- Obtaining project approval

It is advisable at this stage to include an arrangement for additional processes such as the roles and responsibilities, communications, items to be purchased and the project kick-off meetings.

Delivery: The destination has been conceptualized and the map carefully crafted. The next step in the process is to embark on the journey. This is an arena where social entrepreneurs are generally passionate and are ever willing to work on. It is their cause and reason as to why they began the social enterprise in the first place. Idea generating and map drafting generally isn't their concern. They are 'doers' and easily get frustrated if they fail to make things happen.

The delivery stage ensures that the project deliverables have been executed in accordance to the plan. Appropriate allocation, coordination and human resource management are key players to the success realized in this stage. The victory is measured in terms of whether the project deliverables have been fulfilled or not.

Evaluation: Business activities place us in a position where we have to try out all sorts of techniques as we come in contact with different types of customers. The growth of the social enterprise is determined by our zeal to sit down and review the work undertaken. Each project factor is analyzed, their contribution to the mission, their success and their failures along with a special research on the cause of said failure. Even though evaluation comes at the final stage, it is important to carry out constant assessment of all factors throughout the project in order to create room for changes to the plan if required.

Evaluation ensures that the project performance is closely monitored to spot potential problems so that necessary action is carried out in a timely manner. Evaluation is a process that analyzes the following:

- Activities being undertaken

- The project variables such as scope, effort, and cost (These are monitored with respect to the project plan – where should we be?).

- Relevant corrective actions to get the project back on the appropriate path

- Influential factors that may bring about a change in the project during its implementation

In projects with multiple phases, the appraisal is a great source of feedback from the individual project stages to instigate relevant changes and to ensure that the project remains in line with the plan.

Project maintenance is a continual process. It captures timely updates on the mission. Project auditors at this stage are mostly interested in the speed at which user problems are resolved.

Closing

Closing is the stage where project outcomes have been accepted, and the project is ending. Some administrative tasks here may include archiving of files and documenting the lessons learned. Two things that happen at this stage are contract and project closure.

Contract closure involves the completion and settlement of all the contracts linked to the project. With the agreement issues handled, all activities across the lifecycle are finalized.

The closing phase includes a Post Implement Review. This is an important event that allows the project teams to understand their mistakes as well as identify the causes determining the success of a mission which can be treated as valuable lessons for future projects. It involves appreciating the things that worked according to the plan and analyzing the factors that could have been done in a better manner.

Project Planning and Proposal Development

Project planning entails numerous steps targeted at realizing a given organizational or community goal or a set of objectives. The primary objectives are usually identified through a particular strategy or a community plan. Project aims can be developed from social enterprise goals, and strategies through meetings and gatherings with the community to be impacted.

Project planning is an important element in project management, which is associated with the use of schedules like Gantt charts, which is used to plan and eventually report the project outcomes.

Project planning begins with defining the project scope and the methods necessary to complete the various tasks. With that determined, the duration and the responsibilities to be handled are listed in the work breakdown structure.

Project design is necessary to organize different segments including workload, hierarchy, and team/individuals' management. Tasks that are interdependent are highlighted with the use of an activity network diagram, identifying a clear path for the project.

Project planning comes before the initiation of the actual assignment, making it inherently uncertain. Therefore, the time duration and costs that are written in the plan are only close estimates. The approximation is undertaken via weighted average optimistic, pessimistic and standard cases. It is normal that the entire program allows for potential delays and creates avenues for unknown eventualities. Use of Project Management Software is recommended.

At this juncture, the planner is at liberty to optimize the project schedule to strike a balance between the duration and resource allocation that is compatible with the project objectives. Once project design is in place, the project timetable becomes a baseline schedule. The entire progress will be evaluated on the basis of this baseline schedule throughout the project lifecycle.

Different approaches can be followed in the project planning process. These include:

Comprehensive planning

Comprehensive planning involves the community-wide assessment of needs to identify and prioritize long-range goals as well as barriers that may hinder the achievement of these goals. Once the objectives are defined, the community can be engaged to develop a method through which the long-range goals can be accomplished and discuss ways in which identified problems can be tackled. The proposed method should factor in techniques for measuring progress throughout the project life cycle. Comprehensive plans take as much as a year to complete and may have a lifespan of 5 to 10 years.

Strategic planning

This approach is adopted by the organization when it already has a comprehensive plan and wants to take action toward achieving the long-term goals. Stakeholders are engaged to identify the problems, figure out their solution and devise techniques to achieve said objectives. Strategic planning is a lengthy process, and it could take up to a year to complete a strategic plan.

Social enterprise without a comprehensive or strategic plan

Developing policies and programs can consume a lot of time. They require the engagement of all the stakeholders and the community as well. If an organization lacks both a comprehensive and strategic plan, different methods are available for project planning.

Some alternative methods could be derived from past meetings that documented the different stakeholder's needs. The historical documentation of previous projects, their design, and their goals can be used as a measure of what the current plan should entail. Community assessments are also significant in developing a plan.

Proposal Development

Federal governments, foundations, and private institutions have a defined format that is to be followed for submission of proposals. Most of these organizations have guidelines regarding the content, page limitations, deadlines, and the required number of copies to be submitted.

The most likely format of your proposal will contain the following elements:

- Cover page

- Abstract/Project Summary

- Table of Contents

- Project Description

- Budget and Budget Justification

- Biographical Sketches of Key Personnel

- Resources (equipment and facilities)

- References

- Appendices

- Certifications and other forms required by the agency

In addition to these, it is important to understand the fundamental questions that reviewers ask as they read through the proposal:

1. What is the intellectual quality and merit of the project?

2. What is/are the likely impact(s)?

3. How likely is the project to produce new helpful data?

4. How valid is the hypothesis? Is there any evidence supporting it?

5. Are the proposed project goals valid?

6. Are the identified procedures adequate, appropriate and related to the study?

7. Have the key personnel shown competence, experience and related credentials?

8. Are the current environmental factors and facilities favorable to the proposed project?

The ten steps to prepare for the proposal development process are as follows:

1. Identify that a need exists for such a project

2. Have at hand necessary background information

3. Validate the need

    a. How is the need different from all the other needs?

    b. Why should you be funded and not another organization?

    c. What is the statistical data that supports the need?

    d. Who studied the need and what were the findings?

4. What is your proposal for addressing the need?

5. When do you expect the work to be completed?

6. What are the anticipated outcomes?

7. Are the results measurable?

8. Who will be the project manager?

9. What is your organizational capacity?

10. What are your budget estimates?

    a. Is the staffing adequate?

    b. Is the program sustainable?

    c. Who will provide fiscal oversight?

Project Implementation

Project implementation means activating the actions described in the work plan. Executing the project is not the same as planning it. During execution, one encounters issues that may or may not have been anticipated during the planning process.

For successful project implementation, undertake the following steps:

1. Have the relevant infrastructure within your reach

2. Work hand in hand with the related organizations

3. Implement on-going training

4. Install the production/process solution

5. Change data from one format to another if appropriate

6. Conduct detailed production/process monitoring

7. Make use of new processes and procedures

8. Maintain focus on the solution

Most project plans depend on the assumptions that a project will run smoothly once implementation begins, but this does not always happen. Every project has a set of technical and general issues that may hinder implementation. These include:

- Vague or varying requirements throughout the project lifecycle

- Slow or poor communication between people involved

- Delay in starting the project

- Using outdated techniques to manage the project

- Inadequate skills amongst the teams/team members selected to work on the project

- Lack of accountability, especially when there is no project manager

- Ambiguous Contingency Plans

- Impossible deadlines

- Failure to engage all relevant stakeholders

- Using too much time to solve new problems once the project goes live.

Successful implementation demands proper planning and communication.

SECTION 5: EVALUATION OF A SOCIAL ENTERPRISE

Design, monitoring, and evaluation are the responsibilities of project management. The underlying importance of the project management lifecycle is to support all the stakeholders and ensure forward progress toward achieving identified goals before project completion. It is also vital to validate that the project goals have been met once the project comes to closure.

Evaluation is an activity that should be an ongoing process throughout the project, from one stage to the next. Even though assessment can take place at any given time during the project, the appropriate timing depends on the nature of the project.

There isn't a particular defined method for carrying out the evaluation. The most suitable method is one developed after detailed consultation with the stakeholders. Regardless of the method chosen, the following elements should preferably be included:

- Planning the appraisal

- Gathering information

- Analyzing the information

- Incorporating the conclusions

Some of the evaluation methods that can be used include asking people questions through interviews, surveys, and questionnaires. Physical methods include direct measurements such as photographic records, aerial photographs, and participant observation. Participant observation involves collecting data by watching, listening, and documenting what is seen and heard.

Organizational program decisions and policies can be improved through evaluation of necessities. This process can further lead to an improvement as well as the accomplishment of desired performance. Subsequent decisions – such as design, implementation, and evaluation – are based on the results of the needs assessments.

Assessments are undertaken before an action is taken so that they can provide useful insight into current conditions. They create the core baseline upon which planning can be based. Being an extension of the strategic planning process, the needs assessment aids in the confirmation, transformation or development of a new mission and vision.

Social Need Assessment

Evaluation of social needs is a systematic process by which needs or gaps in society are determined and addressed from the current conditions to the desired conditions. To appropriately identify the need, it is important to measure the existent disparity between current and desired conditions. The primary goal would be to either make an improvement of what is currently available or to correct the deficiency.

The social needs assessment is a vital step in the planning process for any given social enterprise. The results of such an evaluation can be put to use in improving individuals, training/educating, and refining a product or service. It is also a vital tool for clarifying problems and developing effective techniques for solving the problem. With the problem identified, resources can then be used to design and implement solutions. Selling a good product or providing a service to address a societal need is only possible with the availability of relevant data. Practical assessment of requirements only becomes useful once concrete evidence of the best strategies for achieving the desired results has been identified.

With the goals and required resources in place, a needs assessment is a relatively straightforward process.

A Needs Assessment:

- Identifies the problem that exists within the community/social environment

- Identifies the resources required by the organization to implement a solution

- Creates the basis for which funds can be obtained, developed, and used

Other relevant terms:

Evaluations – An evaluation is the opposite of a needs assessment. A needs assessment is undertaken before a project while an evaluation is carried out after a project is completed. Evaluations look into the relevance and adequacy of current activities, events, and programs with a focus on satisfaction, relevance, and effectiveness of the activity.

Focus group – Refers to the target group on which the needs assessments are based. Typically, focus groups are made up of a representative sample of the stakeholders, including project participants.

Surveys – These are a form of data collection method used during the needs assessments process. Different study types include one-on-one interviews, telephone interviews, and drop-off and pick-up questionnaires.

Program Evaluation – This evaluation gathers information regarding the program or a program unit and then aids in future decision-making based on the information.

SOCIAL IMPACT

Social Impact refers to the social effects that any project or other developmental initiative has on the stakeholders. One way of getting a glimpse of the social impact of a project is by conducting a Social Impact Assessment (SIA).

The SIA should be included as part of the overall monitoring and evaluation process because it analyzes the positive and negative impacts of social interventions at every level. The SIA is a form of assessment that measures intended and unintended social consequences resulting from policies and programs throughout the life of the project.

The SIA is unique in the fact that it seeks to measure broader impacts on society- a major challenge for any evaluation professional. The SIA incorporates risk and hazard assessment, cultural impact, environmental impact, economic impact, and program policies.

Risk Assessment

Maintaining the safety of any business demands that identified risks be kept under control. Doing so makes it necessary to figure out the dangerous aspects of a program/project and then analyze what measures have been put in place to mitigate the risk.

Risk assessment is about identifying practical steps for controlling risks in the organization or proposed project.

When potential hazards are identified, an organization needs to consider ways in which to control those risks, based on the magnitude, timing, and location.

During a risk assessment, it is important to identify the vulnerabilities that are likely to increase the level of susceptibility to a hazard. Vulnerabilities could be protection systems, process systems, security, building construction and loss prevention programs.

To curb the impacts of such vulnerabilities, it is advisable to invest in mitigation. Where the potential for a significant impact exists, a mitigation strategy should be a top priority.

The stages of undertaking a risk assessment are:

- Identifying the risk

- Assessing the risk

- Mitigating the risk

- Contingency Assessment

Risk assessment is an ongoing process, which makes it a vital part of project management and monitoring.

Risk Identification - This is the initial step in risk assessment and involves identifying risks associated with the organization or project management. One way to recognize risks is to make use of brainstorming. This stage only concentrates on identifying and analyzing potential threats.

The average social enterprise may think of risks along the following lines: IT, finance, premises, client service levels, health and safety, volunteer and paid staff, funding, organization, and trustees.

Each of the areas may be associated with different types of dangers of varying magnitude. For instance, risks in the financing area may have to do with the loss of capital, late payments or loss of a significant contract/grant.

After identifying the risks the project or organization is exposed to, the next step would be to review the list and make sure all-important areas are covered, and any overlaps removed.

Risk assessment - This stage rates the threats, based on two factors: impact and probability. Impact risk assessment involves investigating what the potential threat is likely to do to the organization, client or project. The impact could be low, medium, or high.

Probability risk assessment looks into the likelihood of the risk occurring. Just like the impact aspect of risk assessment, the probability can be categorized into high, medium, and low probability.

Risk Mitigation - This stage deals with how to manage the identified jeopardies, starting with the higher and most important ones. There are cases where the only action would be to observe the recognized hazard and see if it becomes significant.

Some risk mitigation efforts include defining steps to take in the event of a given danger, insuring against high-impact risks and redefining the activities that increase the probability of it occurring. After these actions are identified, it is necessary to estimate the resources, costs, and workload of each action.

Contingency Assessment - This is the final stage in the risk assessment process. It has to do with formulating the contingencies required to guarantee project management and performance security. Contingency assessment factors in four aspects: performance, timescale, cost, and funding.

When an organization describes what they do, who they collaborate with, in addition to the impacts they have on society, the benefits, and lessons learned, what they are basically doing is listing the outcomes.

Most social entrepreneurs set out on ambitious projects funded by different investors and donors. When the project reaches its final stage, it is paramount to report to the funding bodies to increase the chances of future funding.

The benefits of having an understanding of the project outcomes:

- Motivates the staff, stakeholders, and loyal customers

- Saves time and money

- Provides clarity concerning work allocation, shared tasks, and administrative hierarchy

- It helps with quality assurance

- It results in more useful information systems

The outcomes of the project have a tremendous impact on future decision-making.

Other factors that influence present and impending decisions include experience, cognitive biases, age, individual differences, and belief in personal relevance as well as an escalation of commitment.

People are faced with different choices every day from which they have to make a decision. In most cases, the decision-making process is precisely determined by the decision being made. Some decisions are more straightforward while others require complex reasoning.

COMMUNITY PARTICIPATION

Involving members of a given community in the projects designed to impact their lives is known as community engagement. It is not advisable to force people to engage in a particular project that directly or indirectly has a bearing on their lives, however, the community members should be given an opportunity to get involved.

There are various aspects of a project during which community participation may be useful. These include the needs assessment, planning, mobilizing, training, implementing, and monitoring and evaluation.

People may be willing to participate in the given project for the following reasons:

- Need to feel a sense of belonging in the community

- Traditional, religious or social obligations for mutual help

- Genuine desire to participate

- Money incentives

EPILOGUE

Social entrepreneurs are going on to become the forerunners of social transformation, augmenting the quality of life and elevating human existence around the globe.

In this book, we have noted the importance of a social venture, the hurdles that a social entrepreneur may face, and suggestions, as well as solutions that are vital to overcoming those barriers.

Social entrepreneurs often become involved in ambitious projects, with certain objectives in mind, but their success depends largely on effective project management practices. Since most social enterprises require continual financial backing, seeking investors to fund the projects is inevitable. The kind of proposal submitted may or may not lead to the acquisition of the necessary capital so such social enterprises should always be prepared to find ways to earn a secondary income.

Social entrepreneurship is a noble mission for any given organization. It can be used by both for-profit and non-profit organizations to pursue their mission. Funding is often a key aspect of these initiatives and marketing plays a significant role in reaching the targeted audience, which in turn should translate to more funds for successful organizations.

Modern societies are relying on social entrepreneurs to tackle public issues which are left unaddressed by governments and NGOs, which means that the field of social entrepreneurship will grow in the years to come.

www.ingramcontent.com/pod-product-compliance
Lightning Source LLC
Chambersburg PA
CBHW070810210326
41520CB00011B/1901